PEOPLE MANAGEMENT AND DEVELOPMENT

CIPD REVISION GUIDE

David Farnham is the CIPD Chief Examiner for People Management and Development and played a significant role in the development of the latest set of Professional Standards. He is also Professor of Employment Relations at the University of Portsmouth.

Paul Smith is a Senior Lecturer in HRM at the University of Westminster Business School. He has a wide range of experience of teaching on CIPD courses and is also a CIPD External Examiner.

The Chartered Institute of Personnel and Development is the leading publisher of books and reports for personnel and training professionals, students, and all those concerned with the effective management and development of people at work. For details of all our titles, please contact the publishing department:

tel: 020-8263 3387

fax: 020-8263 3850

e-mail: publish@cipd.co.uk

The catalogue of all CIPD titles can be viewed on all the CIPD website:

www.cipd.co.uk/bookstore

PEOPLE MANAGEMENT AND DEVELOPMENT

CIPD REVISION GUIDE

DAVID FARNHAM
PAUL SMITH

Chartered Institute of Personnel and Development

Published by the Chartered Institute of Personnel and Development,
CIPD House, Camp Road, London, SW19 4UX

First published 2003

Design by Pumpkin House, Cambridge

Typeset by Pumpkin House, Cambridge

Printed in Great Britain by The Cromwell Press, Trowbridge, Wiltshire

British Library Cataloguing in Publication Data
A catalogue of this manual is available from the British Library

ISBN 1 84398 015 0

The views expressed in this manual are the authors' own and may not necessarily reflect those of the CIPD.

The CIPD has made every effort to trace and acknowledge copyright holders. If any source has been
overlooked, CIPD Enterprises would be pleased to redress this for future editions.

Chartered Institute of Personnel and Development,
CIPD House, Camp Road, London, SW19 4UX

Tel: 020 8971 9000   Fax: 020 8263 3333

Email: cipd@cipd.co.uk   Website: www.cipd.co.uk

Incorporated by Royal Charter.   Registered Charity No. 1079797

CONTENTS

PREFACE

The purpose of this CIPD Revision Guide is to provide suggested learning, revision and examination guidance to Chartered Institute of Personnel and Development (CIPD) students sitting the People Management and Development (PM&D) standard of the Institute. It takes account of the fact that CIPD students often study on a part-time rather than a full-time basis. This CIPD Revision Guide is aimed at these sorts of individuals whose time is limited and is at a premium. Normally, in addition to their professional studies, part-time CIPD students have got jobs to do, homes to manage and families to care for. Their time is precious and they need to manage their learning and revision in an effective way. This CIPD Revision Guide seeks to help them in this task.

It therefore provides systematic guidance to such students on how to study and revise this standard. This is to enable them to demonstrate to the Chief Examiner and his marking team that they can respond to PM&D examination questions in a relevant, persuasive and convincing manner.

In this CIPD Revision Guide, the authors, Professor David Farnham, Chief Examiner PM&D, and Paul Smith, Senior Lecturer at the University of Westminster, also offer advice to students on how to apply the learning acquired during their course of study so as to pass the examination paper. Both authors have extensive experience in teaching and examining in this field of study at postgraduate level, so they are able to write this CIPD Revision Guide from this dual perspective. Following this Preface are five text chapters.

Chapter 1 provides general examination guidance. It introduces the concepts and competencies that underpin the CIPD's Professional Standards, thus enabling Professional Development Scheme (PDS) students to successfully prepare for and complete their examinations.

Chapter 2 outlines the PM&D Standard, by providing an overview of the core PM&D Standard and the field to which it relates. Relevant Performance Indicators and Indicative Content are outlined.

Chapter 3 contains two PM&D examination papers for students to use in preparing for their examination. The first is the exam paper set in May 2003. The second is a specimen paper that was written before the introduction of the PDS in 2002 and was aimed at providing guidance to students and tutors regarding the expectations of the PDS scheme.

Chapter 4 gives some brief feedback and advice on each of the questions included in the May 2003 and the specimen paper presented in the previous chapter. These are not 'model' answers but guidelines on how these questions might be approached.

Chapter 5 draws briefly upon the Chief Examiner's report on how to prepare effectively for the PM&D written examination paper.

We hope that you enjoy your studies and we wish you good luck in the examination. By following the guidance presented here, you should be able to gain the most benefit when preparing, revising and taking the PM&D examination.

Professor David Farnham, Chief Examiner: People Management and Development

May 2003

● GENERAL EXAMINATION GUIDANCE

■ Introduction

The purpose of this chapter is to introduce the concepts and competencies that underpin the CIPD's Professional Standards, thus enabling Professional Development Scheme (PDS) students to successfully prepare for and complete their examinations.

■ CIPD's Professional Standards

The CIPD's new revised Professional Standards were produced in 2001 after a two-year consultation period. They aim to incorporate developments in the practice of people management, and in the thinking that underlies these, since the previous standards were introduced.

The standards are an articulation of the knowledge and competence required to undertake a professional personnel or training and development role. They aim to define 'What is a CIPD Professional?' The Institute has defined standards across the whole spectrum of personnel and development, taking into account both specialist and generalist functions.

The People Management and Development examination tests students against the Institute's revised Professional Standard for that field. Students need to be familiar with this Standard. Chapter 2 of this CIPD Revision Guide also provides a detailed review and analysis of the main points of the PM&D Standard.

Key concepts and competencies

A number of key concepts underpin the CIPD's standards.

The first concept is that of the 'thinking performer'. In essence, those who fulfil the standards must be capable of thinking, at both an operational and strategic level, and they must be able to put this into practice in performing at the business unit level.

CIPD candidates demonstrate competence as *thinking performers* when they show the following:

- understanding of organisational strategy and of the influences on strategy, both internal and external

- thinking that is not limited to their own organisational level

- ability to produce plans that will effectively implement strategy at the operational level

- ability to evaluate the implications of their recommendations for action, thus ensuring that those recommendations are feasible and suit the needs of that particular organisational context

- knowledge of current thinking, in terms of research and general organisational practice, to inform their views.

The second concept is that CIPD professionals should be able to fulfil the role of 'business partner'; they must be capable of adding value to their employing organisations.

CIPD candidates can indicate their competence to act as *business partners* when they show awareness of the need to:

- ensure understanding of key personnel and development (P&D) issues facing the organisation, at all levels

- work in collaboration with internal stakeholders in order to achieve P&D goals

- actively network to increase knowledge of the general business environment, and to inform and support their own professional activity

- be fully informed about the P&D implications of internal and external changes affecting the organisation

- keep up to date with developments in P&D, gather data and share knowledge, identifying ways in which P&D initiatives can add value to the business.

In addition, the aim of the standards is to produce CIPD members who are able to display a mix of the following 'ten competencies':

- Personal drive and effectiveness

- People management and leadership

- Business understanding

- Professional and ethical behaviour

- Added-value result achievement

- Continuing learning

- Analytical and intuitive/creative thinking

- 'Customer' focus

- Strategic thinking

- Communication, persuasion and interpersonal skills.

Students studying People Management and Development need to relate the 'business partner' and 'thinking performer' concepts to their studies and assessments, and be aware of the requirements in terms of the development of competencies. Thus, in the examination, for example, where relevant, do their answers display an understanding of the needs of that particular business? Do their recommendations 'add value'? Can they display a questioning attitude and display analytical thinking? Are they capable of taking a 'helicopter view' and rising above the day-to-day detail to show strategic awareness? Can they transmit their ideas on paper in a logical and coherent form that is persuasive and is directed towards the target audience?

The standards are not therefore to be seen as dry concepts or merely lists of words and phrases – they need to be interpreted and applied to the organisational realities that student practitioners face in their own employment and to other settings. Similarly, the requirement for students to display analytical and creative thinking should be applied to the standards themselves, and to the concepts that underpin them: how are they relevant and applicable?

The two main concepts of the *thinking performer* and *business partner*, and the *ten* associated *competencies* can be seen as the required *outcomes* from the standards, ie what practitioners should be able to demonstrate as CIPD professionals. Although they are specifically relevant to practitioners, they should also inform students' deliberations. In addition to these, there is the *BACKUP framework*, five competencies that are linked specifically to the PDS assessment system. The five competencies are as follows: Business focus, Application capability, Knowledge of subject, Understanding, and Persuasion and Presentation skills. These are five competencies that students should specifically be able to demonstrate during the course of their studies and in their assessment. These five are briefly reviewed below:

Business focus

This is the ability to make value-added contributions to corporate purposes. Students need to show an understanding of the needs of the business in recommendations that they make. Business focus also means that existing ways of doing things need to be evaluated against the criteria that they should add value.

To assist students in developing this competency, it is a good idea if they share information and work collaboratively with other students as well as collecting information and asking questions within their own organisations. This helps to widen knowledge and understanding of the extent to which different organisations demonstrate such a business focus among the people who work for them, both generally and in HR. It is also a good idea to search the literature and Internet for examples of organisations who have world-class reputations for delivering top performance through people. Such cases can usefully be used to illustrate exam answers.

Application Capability

This refers to the ability to develop and present practical cost-effective solutions to problems that are relevant to the particular circumstances faced by an organisation. It is tested particularly in Section A of the PM&D paper, but can also be relevant to certain of the questions in Section B.

In the examination, any recommendations need to show a direct link to the problem or issue under consideration, be sufficiently detailed to convince the examiner of the student's knowledge and understanding of the area in question, and be clearly justified and show awareness of costs and benefits.

One way for students to develop this competency is, in study groups, to address past Section A questions and then for each group to present their recommendations to the rest of the cohort – for feedback and constructive criticism!

Knowledge of subject

Knowledge of the subject matter forms a basis for the other competencies and is vital to successful performance in the examination. Students should make sure that the material in the whole syllabus is understood, at least to the extent of being able to provide short paragraph-length answers to the questions in Section B of the PM&D

exam. For Section A, in addition to the in-depth knowledge they need to answer their chosen question, students must also be able to demonstrate a holistic appreciation of HRM and its contribution to organisational performance. Students are therefore advised to have a broad familiarity of the Indicative Content in general, and a more in-depth familiarity with approximately 50 percent of it.

In terms of reading, *People Management and Development* by Marchington and Wilkinson (CIPD) forms a suitable core text. This can be supplemented by making reference to other general HR/personnel texts, of which there are a wide variety, including those by Armstrong, Torrington and Hall, and Bratton and Gold. The CIPD texts that support each of the generalist electives (Resourcing, Learning and Development, Relations, and Reward) also provide useful material. Students also need to keep up to date with developments in PM&D, by reference to the *People Management* publication, or its online equivalent. The CIPD website also provides an invaluable source of information, and a summary of relevant research reports.

Understanding

Although an adequate level of knowledge of the subject matter is an essential prerequisite for successful exam performance, it is not in itself sufficient. Students also need to demonstrate a critical understanding of what they have learned. For most questions, students are required to move beyond the descriptive to provide explanation, analysis and evaluation. It is therefore important for students to adopt a questioning attitude, to their reading, to their own organisation's approach to HR, and to examination questions.

Persuasion and Presentation skills

Examiners appreciate that for the PM&D Section B questions, candidates have little time in which to produce perfectly structured answers if they are to produce seven answers within an hour. However they should aim at a minimum to write clearly and concisely. Within Section A, where one question is chosen from four, it is more important to structure the answer clearly. It is also vital that the answer is produced in the format requested (report, briefing notes, etc).

In general, students need to: address the question posed; choose from alternatives to formulate a realistic answer; justify and cost recommendations; and write in a clear and well-structured manner that succeeds in convincing the reader. Where appropriate, they should also provide examples to support a particular answer and argument. These may be drawn from their own organisation, or one that they are familiar with. Such examples can be obtained from previous jobs, other students, or from the literature and professional journals.

■ General advice on the PM&D examination

Format of the examination

The exam is in two sections, A and B. The time allowed for the exam is two hours plus ten minutes' reading time. Each section is equally weighted, so approximately one hour should be spent on each.

In Section A, students have a choice of *one* from four questions. Each of the questions in this section requires students to carry out an assignment or task with reference to a particular area of HR. The question may require them to relate their answer to their own organisation, or may relate to some other scenario, such as the preparation for a talk to the local CIPD branch. They may be asked to present their answer in the form of a report, or some other format, such as the design of a training programme, an outline for a talk to be presented, or a letter to be written to a newspaper. It is essential that students comply with these instructions. Students who write essays here, for example, will not pass. It is also vital that an analytical and evaluative approach is taken that considers the question in relation to the wider business context and with reference to relevant literature on the subject, and that provides examples of practice in other organisations as appropriate.

In Section B, students must answer seven questions from ten. Again, about an hour should be allocated to this section. Each question is capable of being answered in seven or eight minutes through relatively short answers. The questions can be drawn from anywhere in the PM&D Standard. This section therefore requires students to present the essential information relating to the area of the question in order to demonstrate their knowledge and understanding. By necessity, answers must be concise, but they can be supplemented with illustrative examples and reference to reading that demonstrates students' wider understanding of the issue. As with the previous section, it is crucial that students analyse and evaluate the issue in question rather than merely providing uncritical description. It is also vitally important that all seven questions are tackled.

Revision and preparation

Revision is a necessary evil, but can be made easier with some previous preparation. A suitable core textbook, such as Marchington and Wilkinson, should be purchased and referred to regularly throughout the programme. Key passages can be highlighted and relevant sections drawn attention to by post-it notes. Familiarity with a core text provides a useful basis for further reading in specific topic areas.

It is also useful to have a large ring-binder with subdividers. This can be used to collect and classify relevant articles by topic, such as 'performance management', 'legal updates' or 'equal opportunities and diversity'. These topic areas can be cross-referenced with the relevant sections in the textbook and form a structured basis for revision. Integration of topics can be achieved by linking topics together, applying them to different scenarios, and practising past examination questions.

Revision sessions can be based around particular topics. For each topic, relevant theories/models should be identified and their application evaluated. Relevant authors should be noted and their articles summarised. A similar approach should be taken to the application of research findings and organisational examples.

Thus, taking one topic as an example – the link between people management practices and organisational performance – students may well have relevant lecture notes or class exercises, and should have read the relevant section of the core text. This could form the basis of revision notes. The CIPD website provides research summaries and this area is well covered. Thus students should make note of the key points of, say, the findings of John Purcell's investigations, in addition to those of David Guest and others for the CIPD. Note could be made of relevant recent articles in *People Management* such as that of 15 May 2003 by Purcell and colleagues highlighting how the way in which people are managed has affected the performance of four different Tesco stores.

Armed with the above information, students should be in a strong position to tackle a question on this subject. They should be able to demonstrate knowledge and understanding, and hopefully a questioning attitude that would lead to analysis and evaluation (assuming such an attitude had informed their initial study and revision). They should also be able to make reference to relevant organisational examples. As long as they address the question as set (rather than merely listing everything they know in this area), then they should do well.

Level

The Professional Development Scheme is a master's level programme, which means that students must display:

- A systematic understanding of knowledge and a critical awareness of current problems and/or new insights

- A comprehensive understanding of techniques

- A conceptual understanding that enables both current research and methodologies to be evaluated critically

- Originality in the application of knowledge

- The ability to deal with complex issues both systematically and creatively, make sound judgements in the absence of complete data and communicate conclusions

- The demonstration of self-direction and originality in tackling and solving problems

- A continued drive to advance knowledge, understanding and skills (principally through CPD).

Because the PDS is a master's level programme, it is also essential that students keep themselves informed about research and wider organisational practice. This can be achieved by regularly reading the research columns of *Shine* and *People Management*, visiting the CIPD's research website: www.cipd.co.uk/research, attending events such as those held by the local CIPD branch, and reading the core text and other texts that contain reference to research studies and examples of organisational practice.

The CIPD expects PM&D students to be aware of the key findings of its various research reports, summaries of which are available on the website, but does not expect students to have in-depth knowledge of them.

■ Exam technique

Students need to ensure that they allocate their time correctly in the examination. The ten minutes' reading time should be made full use of. One suggested technique is to quickly 'skim read' the whole paper, and then read through it again carefully, noting key requirements, words or phrases. Equal time (one hour) should be allocated to each section. For the short-answer questions in Section B, approximately seven to eight minutes should be allocated to each of the seven answers. Candidates should avoid the temptation to spend much more time on answering questions that they find easier or know a lot about. Any spare time at the end can be used to check through answers, making any corrections or additions.

Answers to questions should be reasonably structured so that points are made in a logical sequence and the answer 'flows'. This is particularly relevant to the answer to the chosen question in Section A, since it will be longer than the Section B answers. Students may find that sketching out a brief answer plan may help to order their thoughts and to structure their answer, but this should be brief.

It is of vital importance in the examination that students answer the question. The importance of this cannot be stressed too much. Students may be tempted to write everything they know about a particular topic area, or to answer a question as they wish it had been set, but this will not gain them marks. Students must address the question as set. It may help here to underline or highlight the key words in the question.

Where candidates are asked to relate their answer to their own organisation, this can be interpreted loosely as meaning the one they currently work for or one with which they are familiar. This familiarity could have been gained through their own or others experience, or by reading about the organisation in a textbook, periodical article or on the Internet. This obviously applies where a candidate is not currently employed, but is also relevant where a student's own organisation has few or no relevant examples to offer. In answering such questions it is important to give enough information about the organisation selected to enable the examiner to assess the relevance of the candidate's answer to that particular context. It is vital for candidates to show why their proposals or recommendations are suited to that particular organisation.

In terms of length of answer, it is quality not quantity that counts. High quality answers can also be concise. Lengthy answers can fail if they are poorly informed, or not adequately focused. Time is also a major constraint here – for Section B answers, how much can a candidate write that is relevant and focused on the question in seven to eight minutes? This is likely to be between three-quarters of a page and a page, but will vary with the style of writing.

■ Common errors

Some of the main errors made in exam performance are as follows:

- Not answering all parts of a question. If a question is in two parts, then both parts must be addressed.

- Failing to address the question as set.

- Not presenting the answer in the required format for Section A questions. Thus it is common for students to write an essay rather than a report or draft talk when it is a report or draft talk that has been requested. Practising previous exam questions should help here, and if candidates are unsure as to how to present in a particular format they should consult their tutor well before the examination.

- Failing to justify recommended courses of action, or providing solutions that do not suit the particular circumstances of the organisation in question.

- Not providing any detail of costing of recommendations, or the gains that employers might make, when this information is specifically asked for in the question.

- Losing sight of the overall objective of a question and providing an unbalanced answer that devotes too much time to one part of the question and too little on other parts.

- Failing to locate their answer in the wider context, showing little appreciation of national trends or developments in the economy in general, or in HRM in particular.

- Failing to recognise the political realities of organisations and failing to recognise the force of existing cultural norms and traditions when putting forward recommendations. Students need to show an awareness of the fact that not all options are feasible, and that there are likely to be implementation difficulties with suggested recommendations.

- Providing answers that show little evidence of wider reading around the subject and appear to be based on little more than hoped-for common sense.

■ Some final thoughts on the examination

Students should 'aim high', ie rather than aiming for a Pass (50 percent) they should set themselves the personal goal of attaining an examination mark of at least 60 percent. Students who aim for just a Pass face the danger of failing if things do not go quite to plan on the day. In terms of borderline Pass/Marginal Fail candidates, the key question that the examiners will ask in reaching a decision will be whether the candidate is worthy of practising in the professional field of PM&D.

The previous section focused on common examination errors, but it is worth emphasising the fact that many candidates perform well. A clear and focused revision programme combined with good exam technique will lead to success. Affirmation and visualisation are helpful tools in achieving success – affirming that the desired result will be achieved, and visualising the outcome.

■ Conclusion

The purpose of this chapter has been to provide an introduction to the concepts and competencies that PDS candidates need in order to succeed in their examination, and to suggest ways in which these competencies can be demonstrated in the exam.

Chapter 2 focuses on details of the CIPD's People Management and Development Generalist Standard.

• THE CIPD's PEOPLE MANAGEMENT AND DEVELOPMENT STANDARD

■ Introduction

The purpose of this chapter is to provide an overview of the core People Management and Development Standard and the field to which it relates. The relevant Performance Indicators and Indicative Content are outlined.

■ People Management and Development

The professional standards are structured around four fields, of which People Management and Development is one:

- Core Management

- People Management and Development

- Management Report/CPD (to which the concept of the 'thinking performer' is central)

- Generalist and Specialist Electives.

People Management and Development (PM&D) is a compulsory core for all candidates. It forms the spine for the entire Professional Development Scheme (PDS) and CIPD standards.

The new Professional Standards set out the knowledge and competence that it is considered are required of a professional personnel/HR practitioner today. Some of the areas set out in the standards are subject to choice by the individual; choice as to which route to take, and which electives are the most appropriate. PM&D, however, is compulsory. The main rationale for this is that there is a body of knowledge, understanding and competence that all CIPD professionals should have covered and be able to demonstrate, regardless of the type of organisation they work for, or of their current position or role. This would apply whether they work in the public or private sector, for a unionised or non-unionised firm, specialise in one particular area, such as recruitment or training and development, or work in a generalist role.

PM&D thus covers all the key elements of personnel and development in the main generic areas of resourcing, development, relations and reward.

There are a number of other key concepts and ideas that underpin the People Management and Development Standard. These are as follows:

- The concept of integration. Practitioners need to understand how their work is integrated with that of other HR specialists, line managers, consultants and other stakeholders. *Vertical integration* refers to the links between people management and the business strategy. *Horizontal integration* refers to the 'fit' between different personnel/HR policies and practices.

- In addition, it is necessary to consider not only how the different components of HRM at work interrelate with each other, but also the applicability of these in a wide range of different organisational contexts. In simple terms, HRM policies and practices that work well in one setting may not be directly applicable in a different organisational context. Rather than proposing 'best practice' solutions, consideration needs to be given to developing and implementing 'good practice' solutions that are contingent on the particular situation and set of circumstances, and having the ability to demonstrate clearly why this is the case.

- Practitioners need to gain the commitment of other stakeholders, such as line managers or the board of directors, to their recommendations and advice. Clearly demonstrating how these recommendations, advice and solutions can add value for the organisation is key to this.

- Change and change management are an important aspect of the PM&D Standard. Practitioners need awareness of the changing nature of work and employment and the changing responsibilities for the management of HRM, as set out in Chapters 2 and 5 respectively of the Marchington and Wilkinson (2002) text. They also need to be able to demonstrate change management skills, which form part of Chapter 5.

- PM&D provides a springboard for further learning and development. It both provides a basis for the generalist and specialist electives, and for ongoing Continuing Professional Development (CPD).

The above points have important implications for PM&D students. They need to be able to encompass the broad range of subject matter covered and comprehend the linkages and crossovers. Thus while resourcing, development, relations and reward may be studied separately as subject areas within PM&D, their interrelatedness needs to be appreciated. This is partly because many topics straddle two or more subject boundaries. Thus performance management, for example, has resourcing, development and reward issues at the very least; equal opportunities and diversity likewise; and information technology has relevance to many different aspects of PM&D. In addition, from a practitioner's perspective, real-life day-to-day HR problems tend not to come in neatly defined packages. They are more likely to be a messy amalgam of different, and possibly competing or even contradictory, issues.

Secondly, as well as combining and integrating the, at times, disparate elements of a broad subject, PM&D students also need to demonstrate strategic awareness. This is by no means easy, particularly when one's role is at an operational level seemingly distant or distinct from the strategic pinnacle. It is not made easier by the fact that many organisations appear either not to have a clear strategy, or have an espoused strategy that is either poorly communicated or badly implemented.

Thirdly, students need to be able to tailor their recommendations to suit particular circumstances. For example, HR policies and practices that will suit a multinational are unlikely to be equally applicable to a small regional firm.

Fourthly, in the examination, students need to propose solutions that, as well as being relevant, are persuasive, show an appreciation of the cost implications, and are clearly communicated in a relevant format and directed at the target audience. These issues are explored more fully in Chapter 3 on exam preparation.

Fifthly, as well as demonstrating an awareness of change and change management skills, students need to keep up to date with developments in the field and with legislative changes. *People Management*, for example, has a regular update of research news and of new legislation. The CIPD also produces a range of research summaries, fact sheets, surveys and reports, which students need to familiarise themselves with. Much of this information is available on the CIPD website.

The CIPD's People Management and Development Standard

PM&D forms one of the four fields of the Professional Standards. The standards, in total, set out the requirements for a CIPD professional. Each field sets out the particular standards for that field.

The PM&D Standard, like the other CIPD standards, breaks down into three parts:

1 Purpose

This gives the rationale for PM&D as a compulsory core for all candidates and as a spine for the other standards.

2 Performance Indicators

These provide a way of understanding the standard of performance required by those entering the field. There are 14 Performance Indicators for PM&D, which are provided under two headings:

- *Operational Indicators* define what practitioners must be *able to do*.

- *Knowledge Indicators* define what practitioners must <u>understand</u> and be *able to explain*.

3 Indicative Content

This provides more detail, and indicates the level and context. It is on this detailed content that the exam questions are likely to be based, so candidates need to familiarise themselves with this over the course of their studies.

Once again, it should be stressed that the indicators are not meant to be viewed as discrete areas, they will need to be combined and integrated. Exam questions may well cover more than one indicator.

The following section of this chapter contains an outline of the indicators, together with a summary of the requirements and implications of each.

The PM&D Standard's 14 Performance Indicators

Shaping the PM&D Agenda

The first three Performance Indicators can be grouped together under the heading 'Shaping the PM&D Agenda'. They examine how the People Management and Development agenda is shaped by a number of issues and institutions, as well as broader political, economic, social and technological trends. While such issues and trends are very influential, it is important not to view them in a totally deterministic manner. As Marchington and Wilkinson (2002, p18) point out, in the last twenty years changes in the macro-economic environment – especially changes in patterns of employment and in legislation – have clearly affected the nature of the employment relationship as well as the practice of HR. Nevertheless, although such wider developments do have a significant impact, their precise influence is heavily dependent on the specific circumstances in which a particular organisation operates.

The above highlights two of the major themes that were introduced in the earlier sections of this chapter and which those studying PM&D need to be aware of and to apply, both as students and as practitioners:

- Firstly, that although organisations may be subject to the same or similar broad external influences, the specific outcome of these influences will vary according to the particular situation of any one organisation in question and how they choose to react. Thus some firms flourish in a recession while others fail, some choose a cost-cutting strategy while others choose to invest. Furthermore, the broad general influences (economic trends, legislation) will combine with the particular circumstances of specific organisations to create a unique scenario.

- Secondly, HR practitioners need to understand both the implications of these broad and specific influences for HR and the management of people, but also how the choice of HR action can itself have a strong influencing factor. Thus a decision may be made to invest in training and development despite recessionary pressures. In short, there is a need to be both responsive and proactive.

Also central to this section of the standards is the notion of the employment relationship, whether in terms of the direct employment of staff by an organisation, or in the subcontracting of work to external bodies or use of agency staff. Both parties to the relationship (employer and employee or worker) are likely to share commonalties of interest (in the success of the enterprise, for example), but are also likely to have differences of interest (regarding the effort–reward bargain, for example). Thus the relationship is likely to be characterised by both co-operation and conflict, and at times by confusion and contradiction. The balance of power between the two parties is also likely to vary in different circumstances.

The implications for people management of the changing context of work

Practitioners who are effective in the first indicator are able to implement appropriate PM&D policies that maximise the contribution of people to organisational objectives and reflect wider societal needs. Through coverage of the topics outlined in the Indicative Content, they are able to demonstrate an appreciation of the following:

- The changing nature of work

- The flexibility debate, and new organisational forms such as outsourcing and public–private partnerships and the ways in which these are reshaping work and employment relations

- The changing nature of the employment relationship and attitudes towards work, including questions about job satisfaction, motivation and organisational commitment, the psychological contract and work intensification.

These three themes that form the first standard recur in other parts of the PM&D Standards.

For this standard students/practitioners need an appreciation of current labour market and employment trends, with particular reference to the proportion of workers on 'atypical contracts', such as temporary and part-time. Publications such as *Labour Market Trends* form a useful source for such data and they are also summarised, with supporting commentary, in newspaper and HR journal articles. The *Workplace Industrial Relations* series also provides useful analyses. An appreciation of the possible implications for HR of these trends is also needed. This area overlaps with Indicator 3.

An understanding of the flexible firm model (Atkinson, and Atkinson and Meager) is also required, together with an evaluation of the applicability of such models in practice. Students should be able to debate the relative advantages and disadvantages of different types of flexible working, for both employer and worker.

Lastly, students need an appreciation of the employment relationship, and of different perspectives on this relationship. Related to this are people's expectations of work and the psychological contract. What do people want from work? How do UK workers feel that they are being treated by employers? Students should be able to make reference to studies on the state of the psychological contract, such as those by Guest and Conway for the CIPD. Students should also be able to debate such questions as the extent to which employment is becoming more insecure, and whether work is becoming more intensive and people working longer hours.

The above clearly demonstrates the need for students to have an appreciation of current issues, and a knowledge of relevant data and studies. In other words, they need to keep up to date. This section also requires students to be able to question and debate current issues rather than just repeat a particular viewpoint, and to consider the implications of various issues and trends for particular organisations, including their own. It thus forms a good illustration of the requirement to be 'thinking performers'.

The context within which PM&D takes place in terms of government actions, legal requirements and wider societal needs

The first indicator involves an analysis of the way in which the work and employment context provides a backcloth for the practice of HRM. The approach to such an analysis needs to be multi-layered, since the precise nature of the employment relationship in a particular organisational situation will be the result of a combination of both internal decisions and external influences, with the latter being the result of an interplay between local, national and international forces.

The second indicator focuses on the legal framework, and associated institutions. Practitioners must be able to provide accurate and timely advice on the rights and obligations of employers and employees arising from the contract of employment and associated legislation. The Indicative Content encompasses the following:

- The role of the law in shaping HRM at work, including a consideration of European developments

- Individual and collective rights at work

- The role of Employment Tribunals (ETs) and the Commissions, particularly those relating to equal opportunities, racial equality, health and safety and trade union issues.

Once again, the material that forms this particular standard also informs others since the law has an impact on many different areas of HR.

As stated above, practitioners need to have an up-to-date knowledge of employment law and have the ability to apply this knowledge in the provision of relevant advice. Law textbooks such as Lewis and Sargeant (2002) provide more in-depth coverage, and *People Management* and its online equivalent provide timetables of legislative changes, while publications such as the *Industrial Relations Law Report* and *IRS Employment Trends* provide more detailed coverage and cases. The aim of this standard is not, however, to produce legal experts, and practitioners need to be aware of the limits in their own expertise and know when to consult relevant specialists.

Students need to appreciate the direct and indirect impact of bodies such as Employment Tribunals; directly in terms of cases brought before the tribunal, but also the indirect influence in the message these send to employers as to how to deal with disciplinary and other issues. Students also need to show an awareness of the debates surrounding the increased coverage of employment law, such as the 'flexibility versus individual protection' debate.

Economic and institutional frameworks for PM&D

The third indicator requires knowledge of labour market statistics and trends, such as employment and unemployment rates, both in aggregate and with reference to gender and age, and the shift from manufacturing to services employment. It thus overlaps with the first indicator and shares with it the same requirement for up-to-date statistics and information, and the same sources of such information. It also requires an appreciation of the institutional forces that influence people management and development in the workplace. Practitioners must be able to access, use and interpret data from a range of sources. The Indicative Content falls into the following categories:

- Labour market and employment data; national, sectoral and local patterns of labour supply

- Initiatives in training, learning and skills development

- The principal institutions that influence people management and development in the workplace.

The requirement for an appreciation of labour market and employment statistics and trends has already been reviewed above. The second area examines the changing nature of the training system, from its earlier roots in industrial training boards through to Sector Skills Councils (SCCs) and the Learning and Skills Councils (LSCs) as well as a consideration of vocational qualifications (NVQs). The main institutions for consideration are trade unions and the TUC; employers' associations and the CBI; and ACAS and the CAC.

Some relevant questions for students to debate include the current and future role of trade unions; the relevance of social partnerships; and the role of ACAS in promoting good practice. Students need to be aware of recent legal changes that have affected the role of ACAS and the CAC.

The PM&D Contribution

The next three performance indicators can be grouped under the heading 'The PM&D Contribution'. They examine how HR practitioners can make a distinctive contribution to performance.

The role of research and change management skills in organisations

The role of information technology in supporting PM&D

These two indicators are, each in their own way, somewhat different from the others. Indicator 4 is skills-based. HR practitioners are often involved in project work with other managers and achieving outcomes through the actions of other people. Relevant skills include planning and design, communication, interviewing, managing time, accessing, analysing and presenting data using statistical sources and information technology (which encompasses Indicator 5) and persuasion skills. The main vehicle for covering and assessing these skills in the Standards is via the Research project.

In addition, HR practitioners need to be able to implement recommendations for change and overcome resistance to change. Marchington and Wilkinson (2002, pp137 & 139) set out Buchanan and Boddy's five competence clusters required for people to be effective change agents, and Mayan-White's key features and methods of a change management strategy.

Indicator 5 relates to the above in that IT provides methods for accessing, analysing and presenting data. Information technology is also integrated throughout the PM&D Standards, as IT provides a support tool for PM&D.

The nature and importance of ethics, professionalism, equal opportunities and managing diversity

Practitioners need to demonstrate an ethical approach to PM&D. Commitment to certain agreed standards is central to this. The standard examines the growth and development of a specialist personnel and development function and the need to adopt a professional and ethical stance on HR issues. On occasions the HR function has been regarded as the conscience of employers, there to ensure that, in the pursuit of more efficient and productive work, the human dimension is not overlooked. Compliance with legal obligations, and maintenance of mechanisms for employee voice are two aspects of this, yet professionalism should also relate to how organisations can achieve greater success through the adoption of up-to-date and proven HR good practice. The challenge for HR practitioners is often to persuade line managers of the case for this. Equal opportunities and diversity is just one area where professionalism and ethics combine, and where a business case can be made in addition to the moral one.

The Indicative Content centres on the following:

- The growth and development of a specialist P&D function

- Professionalism, the role of the CIPD and Continuing Professional Development (CPD)

- Business ethics and social responsibility

- Discrimination and disadvantage at work; equality management and managing diversity.

Students should be aware of the possible tensions that may arise for HR in striving for business goals at the same time as maintaining professionalism. However, a strong professional and ethical stance can also provide HR practitioners with a potentially distinctive contribution to improved performance.

Students should also be aware of trends in the provision of family-friendly policies by firms, and be aware of recent, current and proposed legislative developments in this and related areas.

Integrating the PM&D Contribution

The next four standards are based around the concept of integration – the integration of the PM&D contribution in order to deliver higher levels of organisational performance.

Strategic management and its implications for HRM

The need for students to be able to show strategic awareness has already been highlighted as one of the key requirements of the PM&D Standards. This can prove to be a challenge when working at an operational level. To overcome this difficulty, students need to gain an appreciation of the strategy process and of the different theoretical approaches to strategy, as well as an understanding of why organisational reality may be very different. Such an insight should engender the ability to produce practical recommendations as to how to begin to implement strategic plans at their own organisational level. This is the key; PM&D practitioners need to be able to contribute to the effective implementation of policies that are appropriate for that particular business and which contribute to the achievement of corporate goals. In summation, what HR does needs to help the organisation achieve its ultimate goals, and HR needs to be able to demonstrate this.

The Indicative Content covers the following areas:

- Corporate and business strategy; different models and approaches

- Human resource management as a driver, as strategic partner and as an agent of implementation

- The resource-based view of the firm and implications for PM&D.

This standard requires an understanding of different approaches to corporate and business strategy. Students also need to demonstrate an understanding of the possible roles for HR: in leading strategy formulation itself, in acting as a strategic partner, or in simply acting as an agent of implementation.

The integration of different aspects of personnel and development

The Indicative Content of this standard covers the following:

- The link between organisation strategy and HR strategy; vertical integration and 'best fit'

- Converting organisational and HR strategy into practice; blockages and barriers to implementation and overcoming these

- Horizontal integration and 'best practice'; integration of different elements of PM&D.

This standard is closely linked to the previous one. It further develops the possible links between the strategy of the organisation on the one hand, and HR policies and practice on the other. Such linkages are referred to as 'vertical integration'. This encompasses the notion of 'best fit', or contingency. As such it provides a theoretical explanation as to why, in practice, HRM in, say, a leading pharmaceutical firm is likely to differ from that in a small textile factory. It thus provides a useful contrast to ideas of 'best practice'. These ideas are further developed in the following standard. The difficulties involved in these linkages, and in converting strategy into practice, are also explored.

As a corollary to the concept of vertical integration, the standard also encompasses ideas of *horizontal* integration. In relation to PM&D, this refers to the extent to which different HR policies link to, and are consistent with, each other. This is of particular significance to the People Management and Development Standard. PM&D covers the main generic areas of personnel/HR: resourcing, development, relations and reward. The argument propounded in this standard is that, in any one organisation, the policies and practices in these areas need to be consistent, ie that the total is more than the simple sum of the parts. An example of *lack* of 'fit' would be an individual performance pay approach to reward, at the same time as trying to engender teamwork.

The notion of horizontal integration leads on to that of 'bundles' of human resource practices, ie a set of practices that, in isolation, mean little, but in coherent combination become powerful drivers of organisational performance. From here it is but a short step to proposing 'bundles' of 'best practice'. Best practice or high commitment models of HRM propose that it is possible to identify a set of human resource practices that consistently deliver higher levels of organisational performance. These ideas are revisited in Standard 10.

The implementation of HRM: changing responsibilities

HR specialists can take on a variety of different possible roles. Students need to be familiar with the different models of the HR function (Legge, Tyson and Fell, Storey etc) and their application. Within the broad context of 'people management' there is also the associated question as to what should be the preserve of HR specialists, and what should be undertaken by line managers. Several surveys (such as Hutchinson and Wood, 1995) have pointed to line managers gaining increased responsibility for HR issues, particularly in relation to practical implementation rather than policy formulation. PM&D practitioners need the ability to work with line managers, both in a supportive role and more proactively in suggesting initiatives.

Other trends have seen a number of organisations increase their use of HR consultants, and the delivery of HR through shared services and in some cases call centres. Outsourcing HR either partially or completely is another possibility.

The above raise a number of important issues and questions relating to how HR can and will be delivered and to the future of the HR function as traditionally viewed.

The Indicative Content covers the following:

- Line managers and PM&D, implications of devolvement of HR activities

- Consultants and PM&D

- Different ways of organising and delivering the HR function, including outsourcing.

The contribution of PM&D to organisational success

The previous standard raised questions about the organisation and delivery of HR in organisations. Such questions, in parallel with business pressures, have led to the need for HR departments to justify their existence and demonstrate how they 'add value'.

One way of increasing the likelihood that organisations take HR issues seriously, and thus arguably enhance the contribution of the function, is to have a specialist personnel presence on the board. In terms of assessing the effectiveness of HR, one method is to ask key stakeholders in the organisation for their views. Such 'customers' may include line managers, chief executives, or employees. It is difficult for HR professionals to measure the effectiveness of their own function directly, particularly given that their contribution to organisational goals is mediated through line managers. Two possibilities, however, are to carry out benchmarking exercises, and secondly to focus on internal evaluations – by drawing up service-level agreements, for example, or using a range of quantitative and qualitative data.

Lastly, the link between HRM – and in particular, 'best practice' high commitment HRM – and performance has now become a major research area. In the UK this includes work by David Guest and his colleagues for the CIPD. Although questions remain concerning the research itself and the specific mix of HR practices required, there is now growing evidence for a strong correlation between people management and business performance.

The Indicative Content for this standard covers the following:

- Evaluating the HR function, techniques and difficulties

- Gaining support for P&D interventions

- The contribution of HR practices to business performance.

PM&D in Practice

The last four standards are concerned with PM&D in practice and cover people resourcing, learning and development, employee relations, and employee reward. These should be studied and applied in the context of the previous ten standards. Thus, to what extent is a proposed practical intervention likely to 'add value'? How does it integrate with other HR practices, and with the HR and overall strategy of the organisation? How can it best be delivered and evaluated? The four standards are briefly reviewed below.

Effective recruitment, selection and performance management

This standard focuses on cost-effective recruitment and selection, and managing performance for added value. The Indicative Content covers the following:

- Human resource planning

- Recruitment and selection methods and their application

- Induction and employee socialisation

- Performance management and appraisal

- Managing poor performance, and attendance management.

As a result of this standard, practitioners need to be able to implement cost-effective processes for recruiting and retaining the right calibre of staff.

Effective learning and training

This standard focuses on how effective learning and training can contribute to enhanced employee skills and organisational performance. The Indicative Content covers the following:

- Individual learning; learning styles

- Organisational learning and the concept of the learning organisation

- The training cycle and its application

- Evaluating the effectiveness of training events and learning processes.

As a result of the standard, practitioners should be able to contribute to the design, development and delivery of learning and training and to utilise measures to evaluate their effectiveness in supporting organisational goals.

Effective employee relations

This standard examines how effective employee relations can contribute to increased employee potential and commitment. The Indicative Content covers the following:

- Structures and processes for effective employee relations

- Differing approaches to the management of employee relations

- Resolving differences: grievance and disciplinary handling, bargaining

- Gaining employee commitment: communication and employee voice.

As a result of this standard, practitioners should be able to work in partnership with other stakeholders to develop procedures and processes that enhance the commitment of employees and resolve conflict at work.

Effective reward management

This standard covers how effective reward management practices can contribute to enhanced employee motivation and satisfaction at work. The Indicative Content covers the following:

- The role of reward in the motivation of staff

- Different methods of pay and reward

- Equity and fairness in reward

- Harmonisation and non-financial rewards and benefits.

As a result of this standard, practitioners should be able to provide advice about how to motivate and reward people so as to maximise employee contributions to organisational performance.

The last four standards and their supporting Indicative Content have been briefly outlined above. It should be noted, however, that they should not be seen in isolation but integrated both with each other, and with the preceding ten. The discussions that informed the other standards should also be applied to these. There is also the requirement to keep up to date with developments in the four areas of resourcing, learning and development, relations and reward.

■ Conclusion

The aim of this chapter has been to provide an overview of the People Management and Development Standard and the field to which it relates. Detail has been provided of the relevant Performance Indicators and Indicative Content that students will need to be familiar with when preparing for their examinations.

The next chapter provides some general examiner comments based on the May 2003 examination.

• GUIDANCE TO CANDIDATES FROM CIPD EXAMINERS

This chapter outlines some of the basic things that students need to do in order to pass the written examination.

■ The essentials

1 Read as widely as you can during your period of study. Do not just rely upon the core text but draw upon relevant academic journals, professional journals and recognised websites. This will enable you to take account of different viewpoints, competing perspectives and research findings. Keep abreast with current developments.

2 Make sure that you have a good working knowledge and understanding of the PM&D Professional Standards. Work through them, read around them and continually review them.

3 When revising, practise 'model' answers, basing these questions on previous diets of examinations. If you are studying at a recognised centre, do this in collaboration with your peers on the course/programme. You will be surprised how much you can learn together, in study groups.

4 Manage your time effectively. Work out times for studying (or revising) particular topics, cover all the topics in the standards and learn them 'actively'. This means making notes, 'working things out' and 'working things through'. Do not just read 'passively': you will fall asleep! Find out your optimum times for studying and for how long you can concentrate. Normally study in sequential, short 'time bytes' rather than long, uninterrupted periods. You will work more effectively in this way.

5 In the examination room, read the questions thoroughly and make sure that you understand what the examiner is asking you to respond to (see below). Be relevant, answer the question set, not the question that you would like to have been asked. Stick to a time schedule to ensure that you answer all the questions that you are required to do.

6   In the examination room, provide justifications to your answers when asked to.

7   In the examination room, write persuasively, authoritatively and legibly.

8   In the examination room, do not 'waffle' around the question set. Identify the issue being examined, respond to it and stick the point behind the question.

■ Some reasons for getting good marks in the written examination

1 Candidates able to demonstrate understanding of the questions set, underpinning knowledge of the topic and ability to analyse and evaluate the research evidence relating to their answers are likely to be awarded high marks.

2 Answers that are well structured, logically presented and carefully argued are likely to be awarded high marks, providing again that the answers are relevant and to the point.

3 Answers that demonstrate effective wider reading and evidence-based research or professional practice are likely to be awarded high marks.

4 Candidates able to demonstrate critical analysis and systematic review of the examination topics are likely to be awarded high marks.

5 Candidates who present their answers strongly and effectively, with appropriate paragraphing or subheadings, as well as a beginning, middle and conclusion to their answers, are also likely to score well in the examination.

■ Some reasons for failing the written examination

1 Not answering the question set (see above)

It is not uncommon for examination students to ignore questions on the paper that they do not like and to answer the question that they would *like* to have been set or been asked. However well these 'questions' are answered, they will receive few if any marks.

2 Ignoring part of the question

Another common reason for failing the written examination is where candidates only answer part of the question set. They drop marks by doing this. This may be because candidates cannot answer this part of the question, because they are running out of time or because they simple forget to complete the answer. But failing to answer the whole question results in candidates losing marks in that question.

3 Factual errors

Where there are factual errors, candidates are likely to fail that question. Normally this is because they lack underpinning knowledge in the field of study, which does not get candidates any marks.

4 Responses that are too brief

Shortened answers generally reveal that candidates lack sufficient knowledge in the field to provide a convincing answer. Again this results in fewer marks being awarded than would have been the case with normal-length answers. Individuals able to write extensively on a topic are much more likely to gain higher marks than are those who cannot do this.

5 Failure to justify their answers

A key attribute of M-level answers is the presentation of solid, convincing justifications to the questions put. Another reason why candidates lose marks in questions is failure to justify their answers effectively, when asked to do so.

6 Repeating the same point in an answer

A common fault of weak examination scripts, especially in Section B questions, is when asked for 'up to five factors', for example, for candidates to repeat the same point more than once, using different language. The key here is for candidates to think widely around the topic and to draw on knowledge gained across the standards in order to provide an effective response.

7 Injudicious use of 'bullet points'

Injudicious use of bullet points, especially in Section B answers, sometimes results in lack of coherence in answers. In these cases, candidates often fail to make effective links between the constituent parts of the question being answered and thereby fail to develop an effective argument to illustrate their answers.

● PRACTICE EXAMINATION QUESTIONS

■ Introduction

This chapter contains two People Management and Development papers for students to use in preparing for their examination. The first is the exam paper set in May 2003. The second is a specimen paper that was written before the introduction of the Professional Development Scheme in 2002 as a means of introducing students and tutors to the expectations of the new scheme.

As part of their preparation, students may like to use either or both these papers as a mock examination by actually attempting them in the allotted time of two hours ten minutes. Alternatively, they may prefer just to work through the papers, noting down the points they would make in response to the questions. Either way, the following chapter gives advice on how to tackle the questions in these two papers.

▪ People Management and Development Examination Paper, May 2003

Instructions

Time allowed – Two hours plus ten minutes' reading time.

Answer ONE question in Section A and SEVEN of the ten questions in Section B.

Equal marks are allocated to each section of the paper. Within Section B equal marks are allocated to each question.

Questions may be answered in any order.

If a question includes reference to 'your organisation', this may be interpreted as covering any organisation with which you are familiar.

You are likely to fail the examination if:

you fail to answer SEVEN questions in Section B

and/or

you achieve less than 40 percent in either section.

Section A

Answer ONE question in this section, making sure that you write your answer in the form of a report, a talk, or whatever you are required to do in the question.

1   Your new Chief Executive has asked you to prepare an internal paper outlining and evaluating how recent changes in the political, economic and legal environment have affected your organisation in terms of its people management and development policies and practices. Draft this document, by identifying the main issues, discussing them and providing any necessary background to your organisation.

2   The topic for the annual management debate at the local branch of the Chartered Management Institute (CMI) is 'Business is business and ethical considerations are not the responsibility of business organisations'. As a leading member of the Chartered Institute of Personnel and Development (CIPD) locally, you have been invited by the Chair of the CMI to oppose this motion. You want to give a good professional and personal impression by accepting the invitation and putting on a convincing performance at the debate. Outline the arguments that you would use and indicate how you will try to persuade the audience to support your case.

3   The local sixth-form college has a lunch-hour business forum for students, where invited speakers talk about 'Current Business Issues'. You have been asked to give a short talk, followed by a discussion, to about 40 students on the importance of the people management and development function in contributing to organisational performance. What will you say and why?

4   The Human Resources (HR) Director has asked you to critically review the appraisal system for a specified group of staff within your organisation. Drawing on recent research in the field, and your knowledge of other organisations, discuss how this appraisal system might be changed to improve organisational performance. Indicate what those improvements might be.

Section B

Answer SEVEN questions in this section. To communicate your answer more clearly, you may use whatever methods you wish – for example diagrams, flow charts, bullet points – as long as you provide explanations with these.

1   Identify the main types of flexible employment practices that have been introduced into your organisation in recent years. Explain why this has or has not happened and assess their impact on organisational effectiveness.

2   You have been asked by the head of people management and development to undertake a salary survey of secretarial staff in your locality. Outline what you would aim to do, how you would do it and why.

3   Various researchers have identified a number of models of the human resources/people management and development function. Identify **one** of these models and critically assess its usefulness as a tool for understanding the complexity of the function. How does this model relate to your organisation?

4   Organisations are increasingly using external management consultants to undertake people management and development activities for them. Explain why this is happening and justify a list of suitable criteria by which such consultants might be selected. Give examples from your organisation where appropriate.

5   Identify the most common forms of recruitment methods used in your organisation. Assess how far they are cost-effective.

6   Evaluate the factors leading to the growth of performance management systems in organisations. What is the evidence that such systems add value to organisations?

7   Given the many criticisms of Investors in People (IiP), how can an organisation use IiP to best advantage?

8   Critically review the role of trade union learning representatives in workplaces.

9   What are the major problems managing employee grievances? Drawing on evidence from your organisation, what are some of the problems in operating such a procedure? How would you overcome these problems?

10 What does research on payment by results (PBR) schemes tell us about the conditions under which PBR schemes are likely to be most effective?

■ People Management and Development Specimen Paper

Instructions

Time allowed – Two hours plus ten minutes' reading time.

Answer ONE question from Section A and SEVEN of the ten questions in Section B.

Equal marks are allocated to each section of the paper. Within Section B equal marks are allocated to each question.

Questions may be answered in any order.

If questions refer to 'your organisation', this may be interpreted as covering any organisation with which you are familiar.

You are likely to fail the examination if:

    you fail to answer SEVEN questions in Section B

    and/or

    you achieve less than 40 percent in either section.

Section A

Answer ONE question from this section, making sure that you write your answer in the form of a report, a talk, or whatever you are required to do in the question.

1 Your new chief executive has asked you to prepare an outline paper indicating how people management and development strategy in an organisation of your choice might be integrated with organisational strategy and thereby contribute to improved organisational performance. Draft this paper, providing any necessary background information about this organisation to justify your response.

2 'Assessment centres are neither cost-effective nor efficient in the selection process.' This is the topic to be debated at the local CIPD branch between students on the CIPD course and local people management and development practitioners. Your team, the students, has to decide whether to speak for or against the motion. As team leader, you have been asked by your team to recommend what should be done. Draw up a list of points EITHER supporting OR opposing the motion. Explain and justify the key points your team would make and indicate how you would gain support for your arguments.

3 You have been asked to make a presentation to a group of 30 management students at your local college of further education on 'how employee learning and development can contribute to the bottom line in organisations'. Outline the learning outcomes you want to be achieved, specify what you plan to say and indicate how you will make your presentation an interesting one for the group. Justify your answer.

4 Critically review EITHER the reward management strategies of your organisation OR the employee relations strategies in terms of impact that they have on organisational performance and staff motivation. In the light of this review, make appropriate recommendations on how these strategies might be redesigned in order to improve organisational performance and staff motivation.

Section B

Answer SEVEN of the ten questions in this section. To communicate your answer more clearly, you may use whatever methods you wish – eg diagrams, flow charts, bullet points – so long as you provide explanation of these.

1   Evaluate how changes in the political and legal environment have affected your organisation in recent years.

2   Assess the research skills involved in preparing a report for your chief executive on EITHER the recruitment problems facing your organisation and how these might be addressed OR how induction training in your organisation might be improved.

3   What ethical principles should underpin the activities of the people management and development professional? Provide examples where these principles might conflict with organisational objectives and why.

4   Review three high commitment People Management and Development practices and explain how these may contribute to improved workplace performance.

5   Give examples of the people management and development activities most likely to be devolved to line managers. Discuss how the people management and development professional can ensure that line managers undertake these tasks effectively.

6   In what circumstances are employers likely to use external people management and development consultants rather than in-house resources for advice?

7   Identify the elements of cost-effective recruitment advertising and explain how it can contribute to effective staff selection.

8   Provide examples of self-directed, group-based methods of learning and critically review their effectiveness in contributing to individual and organisational learning.

9   Explain how partnership agreements between employers and trade unions can contribute to effective employment relations in organisations.

10 Under what circumstances is individual performance-related pay most likely to motivate employees?

■ Conclusion

This chapter has provided two examples of PM&D examinations. The CIPD's core text in People Management and Development, by Marchington and Wilkinson, provides other examples of the type of questions that students will face in the exam.

Chapter 5 of this CIPD Revision Guide provides advice on how to tackle each of the Section A and Section B questions in this chapter.

• FEEDBACK ON EXAMINATION QUESTIONS

■ Introduction

In this chapter, brief feedback and advice is given about each of the questions included in the May 2003 and the specimen paper presented in the previous chapter.

If you have written answers or answer plans to these questions you will find it useful to compare what you have written to the feedback provided here in order to identify any gaps and areas for improvement.

No model answers are provided. This is because there is likely to be a range of possible responses to each question rather than definitive 'right' or 'wrong' answers. This is not to say that 'anything goes'! Answers must be relevant. They must clearly address the question asked, show knowledge and understanding of the subject matter, including current research and trends, demonstrate business applicability, and be clearly justified and presented. In addition, many questions require answers that make reference to an organisation that the candidate can specify, and thus each answer will be distinctive.

■ May 2003 Paper

Section A

Question 1

Your new Chief Executive has asked you to prepare an internal paper outlining and evaluating how recent changes in the political, economic and legal environment have affected your organisation in terms of its people management and development policies and practices. Draft this document, by identifying the main issues, discussing them and providing any necessary background to your organisation.

In this question, candidates are asked to prepare an internal paper for their Chief Executive Officer (CEO) evaluating how recent changes in the political, economic and legal environment have affected their organisation in terms of its people management and development policies and practices. This question gives wide scope for candidates to identify those issues most affecting their own organisations. In answering the question, it is necessary for candidates to provide an outline background to their organisation and the external environmental pressures facing it. No area of environmental change is proscribed or prescribed.

Particular changes affect specific organisations differentially. Political changes in government policy, for example, particularly affect public organisations such as the modernisation agenda in the public services, with attendant impacts on people management and development practices. Economic changes, such as changes in fiscal or monetary policy, affect demand for products or services in the private sector and hence impact on issues such as recruitment and selection, human resources planning and managing redundancy. Legal changes arising from either UK employment legislation or that of the EU, such as union recognition, the national minimum wage and family-friendly policies, similarly impact on related people management and development decisions. This question seeks an in-depth answer identifying the main issues, discussing them and analysing them in an organisational context.

Better marks will be awarded to candidates who identify a wider range of issues and how these impact on their organisations. Candidates also need to evaluate and discuss their findings. Good answers will be well balanced between the two main themes – external changes and their impact on organisations. Candidates need to demonstrate strategic awareness and critical analysis. Political, environmental and legal issues need to be discussed in terms of the impact they would have on HR issues.

Answers need to be produced in the form of an internal paper for their CEO. It needs to be clearly written, coherent and provide clear explanation of points.

Question 2

The topic for the annual management debate at the local branch of the Chartered Management Institute (CMI) is 'Business is business and ethical considerations are not the responsibility of business organisations'. As a leading member of the Chartered Institute of Personnel and Development (CIPD) locally, you have been invited by the Chair of the CMI to oppose this motion. You want to give a good professional and personal impression by accepting the invitation and putting on a convincing performance at the debate. Outline the arguments that you would use and indicate how you will try to persuade the audience to support your case.

This question requires candidates to prepare for a debate at the local branch of the Chartered Management Institute. The topic is 'Business is business and ethical considerations are not the responsibility of business organisations'. Candidates are asked to oppose this motion and to outline the arguments that they would use, indicating how they would try to persuade the audience to support their case.

Responses to this question could start with an outline of what the motion stands for, namely that, in free market conditions, the only social responsibility business has is to maximise its profits and it is government's residual task to promote 'good values', if this is supported by the electorate. A major set of arguments against the motion rests on the 'stakeholder' model of business. This suggests that shareholders, employees, customers, suppliers, the community and those with a concern for the environment, all have a stake or an interest in ethical business practices. Ethicality, it is claimed, makes economic sense since an ethical business is more likely to be successful than an unethical one. This is likely to result in improved motivation of staff, better reputation/loyalty with customers and better relations with corporate stakeholders.

Ethicality makes social sense too because, with government providing minimum ethical standards in terms of consumer protection, employment rights and health and safety, many people expect businesses to go beyond minimum legal requirements. Ethicality also balances organisational interests, thus ensuring that no interest becomes dominant. Some examples of good practice in ethical behaviour by model organisations could be provided in the debate. Candidates also need to indicate how they would try to persuade their audience to support their case, in a convincing way.

Recent examples of ethical business practices need to be discussed. Clear arguments would need to be delivered in order to convince what may be a fairly critical audience. Good answers would focus on the subject matter of the debate and take the stakeholder view of the firm to argue against the motion. Clear examples of organisations that operate in a model way in terms of ethical considerations in business would be included.

Question 3

The local sixth-form college has a lunch-hour business forum for students, where invited speakers talk about 'Current Business Issues'. You have been asked to give a short talk, followed by a discussion, to about 40 students on the importance of the people management and development function in contributing to organisational performance. What will you say and why?

In this question, candidates are asked to give a short talk, followed by a discussion, to about 40 students on the importance of the people management and development function in contributing to organisational performance. They also have to justify their answer.

This question is prompted by the search for establishing links between effective people management and development activities and organisational performance, which is now a major research area in HRM. The debate focuses on the works of Guest and others and the role of high commitment work practices as drivers of high performance. This debate is not without controversy but has strong support. The HR activities claimed to enhance performance include appropriate job design, recruitment and selection, training and development, appraisal, rewards, communication, job security and harmonisation practices.

HR performance outcomes include employee competence, commitment and flexibility. Organisational performance outcomes, in turn, are claimed to be connected with quality of goods and services, productivity and efficiency. Candidates are expected to argue that the case justifying the HRM/performance link is based on the claim that the greater the number of HR practices employed by organisations the higher their levels of reported productivity, quality and financial results. The more effectively these HR practices are used the better is organisational performance.

This question therefore requires knowledge of the literature to demonstrate how these HR practices result in improved performance. Answers need to make reference to the work of scholars such as Guest and Pfeffer, the issue of HR bundles and research into the HRM–organisational performance link. This is the key element of the discussion. Good answers therefore need to make clear links to relevant research studies and supporting evidence, as well as raising the critical issues and questions surrounding this area. The arguments need to be of a suitable level and format for sixth-form college students.

Question 4

The Human Resources (HR) Director has asked you to critically review the appraisal system for a specified group of staff within your organisation. Drawing on recent research in the field, and your knowledge of other organisations, discuss how this appraisal system might be changed to improve organisational performance. Indicate what those improvements will be.

This question asks candidates to critically review the appraisal system for a specified group of staff within their own organisation. They are expected to draw on recent research in the field, their knowledge of other organisations, and discuss how this appraisal system might be changed to improve performance.

Answers need to outline these schemes, review them and assess their impact on performance. Just describing an existing staff appraisal scheme is not sufficient. Responses should also discuss some measures of performance that might link with effective staff appraisal schemes in terms of efficiency, productivity, profitability, absenteeism, turnover and so on. Candidates would also be expected to address the issue of what changes in existing schemes might improve performance in these areas. Thus they need to be able to assess and critique their organisation's approach to appraisal. Better answers would include a review of the part that appraisal plays within performance management.

In answering this question, candidates need to make reference to recent research, such as CIPD research reports, and make use of knowledge of other organisations. Clear proposals need to be made for improvement. These recommendations need to be appropriate for the circumstances. Answers need to provide more than merely a description of the appraisal process. And analyses need to be linked to theory.

Section B

Question 1

Identify the main types of flexible employment practices that have been introduced into your organisation in recent years. Explain why this has or has not happened and assess their impact on organisational effectiveness.

In this question, candidates are asked to identify the main types of flexible employment practices that had been introduced into their organisations in recent years. They also have to explain why this has or has not happened and to assess the impact on organisational effectiveness.

Some definitions of flexible employment practices are required, but with reference to candidates' own organisations. There are various ways of defining employment flexibility in terms of hours of work, contractual arrangements and working practices. A more formal framework of analysis could include numerical, functional and pay and outsourcing flexibilities, as per Atkinson. The factors leading to employment flexibilities include product and labour market pressures, government policy and globalisation of international trade. These incorporate sectoral shifts in employment from manufacturing to services, the changing gender distribution of the workforce, extended working hours to meet customer needs and employer needs to maximise use of expensive capital.

Answers to the question also need to assess the impact of flexibilities on organisational performance in the organisations of candidates, doing this by drawing on appropriate examples. All parts of the question need to be addressed, including the impact of such practices, and answers should include a discussion of the factors that have led to an increase in flexible working practices. It is useful to make reference to relevant models, such as Atkinson's, but these need to be applied to the question and not just described.

Question 2

You have been asked by the head of people management and development to undertake a salary survey of secretarial staff in your locality. Outline what you would aim to do, how you would do it and why.

This question asks candidates to undertake a salary survey of secretarial staff in their locality, outlining what they would aim to do, how they would do it and why they would do it. The key part of the question is 'a salary survey of secretarial staff in your locality' and any answer needs to be centred on this requirement.

There are several ways in which this task could be done. Basically, the aim of the research would be to get information on the salaries paid to secretarial staff from local employers in the private and public sectors, in a sensitive manner. A main method of data collection could be by contacting local employers and using either telephone interviews or short postal questionnaires for this purpose. These would seek to provide a cost-effective way of collecting the information, which is both reliable and valid in the circumstances, and would be reported to the head of people management and development services. Better answers will consider realistic primary and secondary research options.

The question has three parts. Thus detail of the method of data collection needs to be outlined and justified against other methods in terms of reliability, cost-effectiveness and validity.

Question 3

Various researchers have identified a number of models of the human resources/people management and development function. Identify one **of these models and critically assess its usefulness as a tool for understanding the complexity of the function. How does this model relate to your organisation?**

In this question, candidates are asked to identify one model of the human resources/people management and development function and critically assess its usefulness as a tool for understanding the complexity of the function. They are also asked how this model relates to their organisation.

A number of personnel and development/HR models could be identified, analysed and explored. These include Legge (1978), Tyson and Fell (1986), Storey (1992), Monks (1993), Shipton and McAuley (1993), Wilkinson and Wilkinson (1994) and Ulrich (1997). No model is preferred but answers need to be related to the candidates' own organisations; thus application needs to be encompassed.

The danger with this sort of question is that, instead of exploring a model and applying it to their own organisations, candidates will merely set out the key sections of the model, describe their organisation and fail to make a link between the two. This would result in answers that are merely descriptive and should be avoided!

Question 4

Organisations are increasingly using external management consultants to undertake people management and development activities for them. Explain why this is happening and justify a list of suitable criteria by which such consultants might be selected. Give examples from your organisation where appropriate.

This question asked why organisations are increasingly using external management consultants to undertake people management and development activities within them. Candidates have to explain why this is happening and to justify a list of suitable criteria by which such consultants might be selected, giving examples from their own organisations where appropriate.

The reasons for outsourcing personnel and development activities include insufficient in-house expertise to deal with a particular project/situation. In some cases external consultants cost less than in-house sources and, despite higher initial costs, management feels the need for an independent/expert opinion not available internally, so that they can help facilitate change. Criteria of selection include expertise, cost and value for money, reputation and a justified reason. Examples need to be provided from candidates' own organisations.

Candidates therefore need to provide a critical review of the use of consultants. Explanation and justification needs to be provided rather than mere description. Once again, the question is in three parts. These are, to repeat, outlining why use of consultants has increased, choice and justification of criteria for selection and providing examples from their own organisations. All three parts need to be covered.

Question 5

Identify the most common forms of recruitment methods used in your organisation. Assess how far they are cost-effective.

This question asks candidates to identify the most common forms of recruitment methods used in their organisations and to assess how far they are cost-effective.

Identifying the methods used should be quite straightforward. Their cost-effectiveness also needs to be analysed. How such costs could be measured and comparisons made should be outlined, as well as the difficulties involved in this. Better answers would draw on other company data, such as the cost of staff turnover, and apply classic correlation measures on method/performance.

Question 6

Evaluate the factors leading to the growth of performance management systems in organisations. What is the evidence that such systems add value to organisations?

This question asks candidates to evaluate the factors leading to the growth of performance management systems in organisations and to review the evidence that such systems add value to organisations. The factors leading to the growth of performance management systems in organisations include increased competitive pressures putting emphasis on performance improvement, attempts to achieve clearer correlation between organisational goals and personal targets, delegation of tasks and responsibilities down organisational hierarchies, and the shift from collectivism to individualism.

Other factors include allowing specifications of individual performance standards and measures and the introduction of performance management processes in the public sector. Added value comes from more effective staff performance, better customer satisfaction and improved organisational performance. Both the external and internal factors leading to performance management systems need to be identified. Once again, all aspects of the question need to be tackled.

Question 7

Given the many criticisms of Investors in People (IiP), how can an organisation use IiP to best advantage?

Candidates are asked in this question to examine the many criticisms of Investors in People (IiP) and indicate how organisations can use IiP to best advantage.

The IiP standard provides a national framework for improving organisational performance, through a planned approach to setting and communicating corporate objectives and developing people to meet them. IiP is claimed to benefit the organisation, its employees and customers in a variety of ways. These need to be explored by candidates. Some of the concerns about IiP are the 'badging' process (ie organisations use it to badge their current systems, not to improve training), failure to engage in best-practice training (ie it is a paper exercise), and weak links between training and IiP. There is also the inability to demonstrate a definitive connection between IiP and profitability and failure to establish links between IiP and staff motivation.

It is important that answers address the concerns about IiP and incorporate them in answering how to get the best out of the standard. Critical analysis needs to be displayed as well as knowledge of the subject matter.

Question 8

Critically review the role of trade union learning representatives in workplaces.

This question asks candidates to critically review the role of trade union learning representatives in workplaces. The role of trade union learning representatives includes generating demand for learning among members, advising about learning, identifying the learning needs of members, negotiating agreements incorporating learning and setting up joint training or learning committees. Other roles include working with employers to introduce and monitor initiatives that benefit members, taking joint ownership of employee development schemes and liaising with providers of training to support workplace learning. Some of the difficulties encountered include reaching a wide range of members/employees, some employer resistance where unions are recognised, and a limited role where there is no union recognition, and problems of small and medium-sized enterprises.

It is important that candidates critically review, rather than just describe the role. Better answers would include an analysis of the recent legislation and accepted practice in this area.

Question 9

What are the major problems managing employee grievances? Drawing on evidence from your organisation, what are some of the problems in operating such a procedure? How would you overcome these problems?

In this question, candidates are asked to consider the major problems of managing employee grievances. They are required to draw on evidence from their own organisations and examine some of the problems in operating such a procedure and how they could be overcome. The objectives of an effective grievance procedure include preventing issues and disagreements between managers and staff leading to major conflict, preventing employees leaving the employer, and establishing a fair and legitimate process for determining grievances. The basic elements of a grievance procedure are that it is formal and written, agreed with employee or union representatives, linked with the procedure to avoid disputes, and issues are settled close to the point of origin. Other elements are the right of employees to be accompanied and ensuring confidentiality of the process. Problems can arise from any of the above elements.

Answers thus need to identify a sufficient number of problems and make adequate recommendations to counteract them. Candidates need to link their answer to their own organisations.

Question 10

What does research on payment by results (PBR) schemes tell us about the conditions under which PBR schemes are likely to be most effective?

This question asks candidates what research on payment by results (PBR) schemes reveal about the conditions under which PBR schemes are likely to be most effective. Basically, PBR attempts to link reward and effort so as to motivate workers. Candidates need to differentiate between individual PBR (eg piece rates) and collective PBR (eg group bonuses). In general, PBR is best used where technological change is slow, quality of output is not an issue, work activities can be measured accurately, standards of performance can be set, and product development is sluggish. As with all questions, it is vital to address the question asked, which includes a consideration of the conditions under which PBR is likely to be effective. Relevant research would include that of Druker (2000), while trends in such schemes are outlined by Millward et al (2000), and authors who have made reference to such research and trends include Michael Armstrong.

■ Specimen Paper

Section A

Question 1

Your new chief executive has asked you to prepare an outline paper indicating how people management and development strategy in an organisation of your choice might be integrated with organisational strategy and thereby contribute to improved organisational performance. Draft this paper, providing any necessary background information about this organisation to justify your response.

This question is concerned with how people management and development strategy might be vertically integrated with organisational strategy within an organisation of the candidate's choice and how this might contribute to improved organisational performance. It gives candidates an opportunity to review the business strategy of an organisation and to comment on the 'fit' between this and its people management and development activities.

In answering this question, it is essential that candidates provide sufficient information about the organisation in question in order to make a persuasive case. Where vertical integration is weak or poorly defined in this organisation, for example, candidates might suggest that achieving fit between business strategy and people management and development strategy in practice is problematic. Much depends on the contingencies of the organisation in terms of its size, structure, market position, ownership and the personalities, skills and expectations of those in top positions, as well as the credibility of people management and development professionals. However, demonstrating the potential contribution of people management and development activities to managing and improving performance through examples of appropriate resourcing, reward, relations and learning and development policies and practices would be a useful starting point in developing an effective dialogue with the chief executive. Where vertical integration is strong, concrete examples of 'good fit' could be identified and evaluated.

The question asks candidates to provide a paper to the new chief executive, and they need to address this in an appropriate way.

Question 2

'Assessment centres are neither cost-effective nor efficient in the selection process.' This is the topic to be debated at the local CIPD branch between students on the CIPD course and local people management and development practitioners. Your team, the students, has to decide whether to speak for or against the motion. As team leader, you have been asked by your team to recommend what should be done. Draw up a list of points EITHER supporting OR opposing the motion. Explain and justify the key points your team would make and indicate how you would gain support for your arguments.

This question is posed in terms of a motion for debate between students and practitioners in the local CIPD branch. Candidates are asked to prepare a list of points either supporting the view that assessment centres are neither cost-effective nor efficient in the selection process or opposing it. They are also asked to explain and justify the key points their team would make to gain support for their arguments.

This question reflects the increased focus in the new standards on the efficiency, cost-effectiveness and appropriateness of recruitment and selection in organisations, as well as the notion of adding value. The basic arguments for assessment centres are well rehearsed, and it does not matter whether candidates argue for or against the motion. The case for assessment centres is their claimed rational, objective and diverse way of assessing job applicants in line with organisational expectations about future job performance, taking into account the candidate's job history. The case against them hinges around time, resources and costs expended on such activities when more traditional methods of selection might produce equally valid or more valid selection outcomes.

Question 3

You have been asked to make a presentation to a group of 30 management students at your local college of further education on 'how employee learning and development can contribute to the bottom line in organisations'. Outline the learning outcomes you want to be achieved, specify what you plan to say and indicate how you will make your presentation an interesting one for the group. Justify your answer.

This question asks candidates to outline a presentation to a group of management students on 'how employee learning and development can contribute to the bottom line in organisations'. It asks candidates to identify their learning outcomes, specify what they plan to say, indicate how they will make their presentation an interesting one and justify their answer. The question reflects the focus in the standards on managing learning processes for organisational success.

The argument to be presented by candidates centres on the role that planned learning and development activities – such as courses, events, assignments and so on – align with organisational objectives and the organisation's business priorities. Such learning and development activities need to motivate trainees and involve line managers in planning learning and development, coaching and mentoring, as well as gaining senior management support to promote learning in line with the dominant corporate culture. The latter objective is more difficult to achieve, but the advantage of this rational approach to learning and development is that it provides a useful framework for developing the presentation in an interesting and participative way. A professional Powerpoint presentation might be used and the presenter could draw on student's own workplace experiences (both positive and negative) to make a more interactive presentation.

Question 4

Critically review EITHER the reward management strategies of your organisation OR the employee relations strategies in terms of impact that they have on organisational performance and staff motivation. In the light of this review, make appropriate recommendations on how these strategies might be redesigned in order to improve organisational performance and staff motivation.

In terms of employee relations, the new standards stress effectiveness, not just a knowledge of processes and functions. The involvement of line management and the value of agreed mechanisms and procedures are also highlighted.

In terms of reward management, motivation is brought to the fore, and choosing appropriate methods of reward. Issues of harmonisation and equality are also stressed.

The question enables candidates to select either the reward strategies of their organisation or its employee relations strategy, critically review them in terms of organisational performance and motivation and make recommendations to improve the system under discussion. Candidates need to specify and describe their existing employee relations or reward system and explore it in terms of its impact on performance and motivation. Reward systems could be examined in terms of their impact on motivating staff, regarding contributions and delivering equity and fairness. Care is needed that recommendations are clearly justified and are appropriate for the organisation in question.

In terms of employee relations, the central issue is the extent to which existing structures and processes – whether in a unionised, part unionised or non-unionised environment – facilitate or fail to facilitate employee commitment and involvement. In either case, in making recommendations for change, candidates need to provide firm evidence for vertical integration of the reward or relations strategy they propose.

Section B

Question 1

Evaluate how changes in the political and legal environment have affected your organisation in recent years.

This question asks candidates to evaluate how changes in the political and legal environment have affected their organisation in recent years. It draws on that aspect of the PM&D standards that refers to the political and legal frameworks in which employing organisations operate. Candidates have a wide range of choice of changes to identify and comment on. Politically, these could include a two-term Labour government, political devolution in Scotland and Wales and developments in the European Union. Legally, this could include recent legislative developments in the areas of flexible working, family-friendly policies, discrimination and consultation. Evaluation of the identified changes needs strong emphasis in answers.

Question 2

Assess the research skills involved in preparing a report for your chief executive on EITHER the recruitment problems facing your organisation and how these might be addressed OR how induction training in your organisation might be improved.

The focus of this question is on research management and change skills, demonstrating the concern of the new standards to reflect the personal and professional skills needed by the people management and development professional to operate effectively in real work situations. These skills include identifying, researching, preparing and presenting a case, and communicating and team-building.

The question is asking candidates to identify and assess the research skills needed in preparing a report to the candidate's chief executive on either the recruitment problems facing their organisation (and how to address them) or how induction training might be improved. It is not about recruitment problems or induction training in general and taken out of context.

In this question, recruitment and induction are being used as a means of getting candidates to identify the appropriate information sources, both internal and external, and the research skills necessary to enable them to make a persuasive written report to senior management on one of these issues. In either case, the sort of research skills that might be identified include: accessing, analysing and presenting relevant data; using statistical sources and information technology; and report writing and presentation skills.

Question 3

What ethical principles should underpin the activities of the people management and development professional? Provide examples where these principles might conflict with organisational objectives and why.

Ethics and professionalism form an important part of the PM&D Standards. This question asks candidates to examine the ethical principles underpinning the activities of people management and development professionals and asks them to give examples where these principles might conflict with organisational objective, and why.

Here candidates need to explore the various dimensions of ethical behaviours within the people management and development function, such as compliance with the law, integrating individual and organisational goals to a common purpose and treating individual employees fairly, consistently and in accordance with agreed rules and procedures. The assumption is that the behaviours need not normally conflict with sound business practice and organisational efficiency. Indeed, positive benefits can accrue from well-designed equal opportunity policies and the management of diversity, monitored by codes of practice and espoused ethical guidelines within organisations.

Candidates might also usefully explore some of the moral and practical issues relating to the management of people and the nature and extent of disadvantage and discrimination in relation to age, ethnic group, marital status, sex and disability. Conflicts between an organisation's ethical principles and its corporate goals can arise in a variety of ways, including poorly codified guidelines and inadequate managerial monitoring of ethical policies. Conflicts also occur where contingent management decisions are taken on purely market or financial criteria and lip service is paid by managers to basic ethical principles to ensure organisational success.

Question 4

Review three high commitment People Management and Development practices and explain how these may contribute to improved workplace performance.

This question requires candidates to describe and review three high commitment people management and development practices and explain how these contribute to organisational performance. The question relates to those parts of the standards that relate to the notion of 'best practice', human capital advantage, horizontal integration, and bundles of personnel and development practices likely to enhance organisational performance.

There is a growing interest in this area, and students would be expected to make reference to the literature that explores the links between the performance management and human resource management cycles. Candidates could then describe a number of high commitment practices including staff development and appraisal, team-working, flexible working practices, job sharing, semi-autonomous work groups, employee involvement and job rotation. They would also need to explain how such practices can contribute to employee commitment, working beyond the contract and enhanced workplace performance.

Question 5

Give examples of the people management and development activities most likely to be devolved to line managers. Discuss how the people management and development professional can ensure that line managers undertake these tasks effectively.

The new standards sharpen the focus on the line management role in organisations and partnerships between line managers and people management development professionals, as well as the possible difficulties involved in devolution. The question asks candidates to give examples of the people management and development activities most likely to be devolved to line managers and how they can ensure that line managers carry them out effectively. The activities that could be identified include selection, appraisal, mentoring, staff development, grievance handling and discipline issues.

The central role of people management and development departments in providing the policies, procedures and systems within which devolution takes place needs to be highlighted, as well as their monitoring role in terms of consistency and even-handedness. But the importance of management and development of line managers, facilitated by people management and development professionals, also needs to be explored and discussed.

Question 6

In what circumstances are employers likely to use external people management and development consultants rather than in-house resources for advice?

The standards examine the role of consultants and outsourcing in people management, looking at the rationale for using and differentiating between consultants and the contribution they make to organisations. This question focuses on the conditions when employers are likely to ask external consultants for advice, rather than in-house sources. The factors to be taken into account include: the relative availability of in-house expertise; the relative cost advantage of external advice; speed of response to organisational needs; the opportunity provided to put contracts out to external tendering and hence get 'value for money'; and the opportunity to draw on external networks for wider professional purposes.

Question 7

Identify the elements of cost-effective recruitment advertising and explain how it can contribute to effective staff selection.

The standards focus on effectiveness, cost implications and appropriateness, and these are reflected in this question. The notion of adding value is also encompassed. For this question, some measure of 'cost effective' needs to be provided, for the purposes of comparison, and what is meant by 'effective selection'. Then the relative merits of the specialist or general press, international, national and local outlets, the Internet and word of mouth could be explored and these linked with expected selection outcomes.

Question 8

Provide examples of self-directed, group-based methods of learning and critically review their effectiveness in contributing to individual and organisational learning.

The standards include a focus on maximising skills and contributions by understanding the nature of learning and searching for a clear picture of why and how learning and development adds value for the organisation and individuals. In line with these changes, this question asks candidates to provide examples of self-directed, group-based methods of training and to review their effectiveness in contributing to individual and organisational learning. Examples that could be provided include learning sets, group-based projects, action learning and video conferencing. These demand varying degrees of monitoring and evaluation but measurement/review of their outputs in line with predetermined targets and timescales, and provision for integrating organisational and individual learning, seem the best way forward.

Question 9

Explain how partnership agreements between employers and trade unions can contribute to effective employment relations in organisations.

This question relates to the contribution that partnership agreements between employers and trade unions can make to effective employee relations in organisations. A definition of partnership agreements and some indication of their variety of form and content is required. Candidates need to show awareness that there is no definitive model template of employer–union partnership agreements. However, their contribution to effective employee relations derives from their emphasis on co-operation between management and union(s), the establishment of single status for all employees, and development of mutually acceptable pay review formulae. Partnership agreements also tend to promote openness on problems and issues of mutual concern and they value good communication, consultation and negotiation. Such agreements aim to avoid disruptive workplace conflict.

Question 10

Under what circumstances is individual performance-related pay most likely to motivate employees?

Motivating staff and rewarding contribution is a main theme of the standards. This question draws on this theme and asks candidates to examine the circumstances under which individual performance-related pay is best suited to motivate employees. It contrasts with the increasing volume of literature that indicates how many employees identify with the principle of such an approach to pay, but criticise its implementation.

These critiques provide the clues where performance-related pay is likely to be more effective in motivating staff. These include: where agreed employee outputs/targets can be effectively measured; where there is a fair and respected system of staff appraisal; where a platform of base pay can be supplemented by known and specific additions to pay; where there is sufficient 'global' money for performance supplements; and where there is a legitimate system of appeal against disputed management decisions.

■ Conclusion

The aim of this chapter has been to provide advice on how to tackle the Section A and Section B questions contained in Chapter 4.

This chapter completes this CIPD Revision Guide. It has aimed to: firstly, provide an insight into the key concepts and competencies that underlie the standards and that are required in the examination; secondly, to outline the People Management and Development Standard and the associated field of study, including details of the relevant Performance Indicators and Indicative Content; thirdly, to provide general examiners' comments on the May 2003 paper; fourthly, to outline the questions in this paper, and in a specimen paper; and, lastly, to provide advice on how to answer these questions.

INDEX

- **NOTES**